THE STORY OF
KING MIDAS

Pamela Espeland
pictures by George Overlie

Carolrhoda Books, Inc., Minneapolis

LIBRARY OF CONGRESS CATALOGING IN PUBLICATION DATA

Espeland, Pamela, 1951-
The story of King Midas.

SUMMARY: Because he speaks without thinking, King
Midas is plagued with a golden touch and the ears of an ass.

1. Midas—Juvenile literature. [1. Midas. 2. Mythology,
Greek] I. Overlie, George. II. Title.

PZ8.1.E83Su   1980   291.1'3'0938 [E]   80-66794
ISBN 0-87614-129-7   (lib. bdg.)

1 2 3 4 5 6 7 8 9 10 85 84 83 82 81 80

to David Porter, who loves what he teaches

ABOUT THIS STORY

Ancient Greece wasn't very big, but it was very important. All together, the Greek states made up an area about the size of South Carolina. From this tiny part of the world came many famous people and ideas.

The ancient Greek people were a lot like us. Over 2,000 years ago, their children played and went to school and watched the Olympic games. Grown-ups worked. They wrote plays and poems. They made laws. Their government was the beginning of Western democracy.

But the Greeks didn't know as much as we do about science. So they used myths to explain nature. When there was a storm at sea, they said, "Poseidon, the God of the Sea, must be angry!" When there was a good harvest, they said, "Demeter, the Goddess of the Earth, must be happy!" Not all myths explained nature, though. Some told about Greek history. And some were just good stories.

The Greek civilization lasted for a long time, but it could not last forever. Around 150 A.D., the Romans took it over. They also adopted the Greek gods and goddesses—they just changed their names to Roman names. (In this story both Greek and Roman names have been used.) Most Romans didn't really believe in the gods, but they did like to tell good stories. So they kept on telling the myths.

Ancient Greece and her colonies shown on a modern map
..... Modern-day Greece

The story of King Midas was written down by a Roman poet named Ovid. Ovid's most famous book is called *Metamorphoses*. The word "metamorphoses" means changes. Each of the poems in the book tells a story about some kind of change. In this story King Midas goes through a couple of important changes. But they don't do him any good. He is not very smart at the beginning of the story, and he is not much smarter at the end.

Long ago there really was a kingdom called Phrygia. It was located in part of the country we call Turkey. And there really was a king named Midas who ruled over Phrygia about 2,700 years ago. So at least that much of the story is true—but no one knows about the rest!

CHAPTER ONE

King Midas was feeling bored. Not much had happened lately in his kingdom of Phrygia. So when he heard his servants laughing and shouting, he wondered what all the noise was about. And he was pleased when one of them ran in and said, "You have a visitor."

What a sight the visitor was! He had pointed ears and a long, furry tail. He had a fat, hairy belly and legs like a goat. There he stood in front of the king, rubbing his eyes and yawning. His name was Silenus. He was an old friend of the king.

"We found him snoring under a rosebush," said the servant. "Drunk, as usual!"

King Midas was not surprised. After all, Silenus was a satyr. And satyrs got drunk a lot. In fact, they hardly ever did anything else. They spent all their time with Bacchus, the God of Wine. They were always having loud parties in the forest. They had had one just last night, and Silenus had drunk too much wine. He had crawled off to take a nap in the king's garden. And Bacchus and the others had gone home without him.

King Midas was happy to see Silenus. They had had a lot of fun together in the old days. So he decided to throw a big party. It lasted for ten days and ten nights. But finally even King Midas got tired. His palace was a mess. Most of his wine was gone. So on the eleventh day King Midas took Silenus home.

"I was wondering where he was!" Bacchus said, laughing. "Thank you for bringing him home. Now I want to give you a reward. Ask for anything."

King Midas was very greedy. He loved gold more than
anything. His treasure house was already full of gold.
But he wanted more. So he knew right away what he
would ask for.

I'll tell you what I want," the king said. "Give me the power to turn anything I touch into gold!"

Bacchus frowned. "That's a very stupid thing to ask for," he said. "Are you sure you don't want to change your mind?"

But King Midas was stubborn. He also had a bad habit. He often used his mouth before he used his brain. He hardly ever thought about what he was going to say before he said it. So now the king folded his arms across his chest and pouted.

"You promised," he told the god.

Bacchus sighed. "Go home, then," he said. "You have what you want."

King Midas couldn't wait to try out his new power. On the way home he touched a green twig that had fallen to the ground. It turned to gold! He bent down to pick up a stone. It turned to gold too! King Midas ran through the forest touching everything in sight. Trees, rocks, dirt, flowers—they all turned to gold!

King Midas had never been happier. He would be the richest man in the world! He would wear gold robes and gold shoes. He would sit on a solid gold throne. He would have a gold bed and a gold bathtub. The other kings would all be jealous of him.

By the time King Midas got back to his palace, he was tired and hungry. Turning things into gold was hard work! So he ordered his servants to bring him his dinner. Then he sat down to eat.

He reached for a piece of bread. He started to take a bite out of it. "Ouch!" he yelled. Something was wrong. Bread wasn't supposed to be hard! Sure enough, when he took it out of his mouth, he saw what had happened. The bread had turned to gold!

Next the king reached for a big bunch of juicy grapes. But before he could even get them into his mouth, they had turned to gold too.

King Midas ran around the table grabbing pieces of food. "Maybe if I get something into my mouth fast enough, it won't have time to turn to gold," he thought. But it didn't work. In a few minutes all his delicious food wasn't food anymore. It was cold, hard gold!

By now King Midas was very thirsty. He picked up a glass of wine and took a drink. Then he spit it out again. Even the wine had turned to melted gold!

King Midas didn't know what to do. He didn't want to give up his new power. But he had to eat! And he would starve if his food kept turning into gold. Finally he decided to go and see Bacchus again. He would have to ask him to take back his gift.

"You stupid old man!" Bacchus yelled. "Now do you see what a dumb thing you asked for?"

King Midas hung his head. He was very embarrassed.

Bacchus started to laugh. He couldn't help it. The king looked so silly. There he stood in his gold robes and shoes. He was wearing so much gold jewelry he could hardly walk. And his stomach was growling!

"All right," the god said at last. "I'll take back my gift. Go to the River Pactolus and wash yourself in it. When you come out of the water, your power will be gone. And maybe this will teach you a lesson!"

King Midas did as Bacchus told him. He washed himself in the River Pactolus. When he came out of the water, his power was gone. Some people say that the sand on the river bottom is still gold today.

CHAPTER TWO

When King Midas got home, he was sick of gold. He never wanted to see anything made of gold again. So he decided to go live a simple life in the country. He moved out of his palace. Instead he lived in a little hut made of grass. He started worshiping Pan, the God of the Fields. He had had enough of Bacchus.

One day Pan and Apollo, the God of the Sun, had an argument.

"Everyone knows how beautifully I play my reed pipes," said Pan.

"But I play my silver lyre so much better," said Apollo.

The two gods decided to have a contest. They asked Tmolus, the Mountain God, to be the judge.

Pan played first. His music was so beautiful that the
birds sang along with it. When he was finished, Tmolus
clapped his hands.

Apollo was next. His music was so beautiful that the birds stopped singing. They wanted to listen too. When he was finished, Tmolus was quiet for a minute. He wanted to remember the tune Apollo had played so he could hum it later.

Then Tmolus said, "I don't understand why you two were arguing. Anyone can tell that Apollo makes the most beautiful music! Apollo wins!"

Now King Midas just happened to be on the mountain during the contest. When he heard what Tmolus said, he was very surprised. Pan was Midas's favorite god. How could Tmolus like Apollo's music better?

The king still had his old bad habit. He used his mouth before he used his brain. He walked right up to Tmolus.

"Excuse me," he said. "I think you are wrong. Pan plays much more beautiful music than Apollo."

Tmolus was shocked. He couldn't believe King Midas would say such a stupid thing. It was stupid for two reasons. First, Apollo really did make the most beautiful music. And second, even if Pan made better music, no smart person would ever say so. Apollo was a much more important god than Pan. It was very dumb to make Apollo angry.

And Apollo *was* angry. He glared at King Midas.

"You must have ears like an ass!" he shouted. "In fact, from now on you *will* have ears like an ass! So there!"

Midas reached up to touch his ears. Sure enough, what Apollo said came true. The king's ears grew and grew until they were long and pointed. Thick, dark hair sprouted all over them. When his ears had finished growing, they looked just like an ass's ears.

This time, though, King Midas couldn't do anything about his big mistake. No matter how much he begged Apollo to change his mind, the god would not give Midas his old ears back. So the king had to wear funny hats for the rest of his days.

Midas was able to keep his ears a secret from everyone except for one person. The barber who cut the king's hair knew about them. But Midas made the barber promise not to tell anyone. And he didn't—not for a long, long time.

But finally the barber couldn't stand it anymore. He just had to tell *somebody*. So he went out into a field and dug a hole. Then he lay down on his stomach. And he whispered into the hole, "King Midas has an ass's ears!"

The barber felt much better after that. He stood up, filled in the hole, and went home. He was sure no one would ever find out what he had done.

But the secret didn't stop there. In the spring, tall reeds grew up in the place where the barber had dug the hole. And whenever the wind blew through them, the reeds whispered, "King Midas has an ass's ears!" Soon everyone in the world knew the king's secret. And the reeds are still telling it to anyone who wants to listen.

PRONUNCIATION GUIDE

Apollo: uh-POLL-oh
Bacchus: BAH-kuss
Demeter: de-MEE-ter
Metamorphoses: met-uh-MORE-fuh-seez
Midas: MY-duss
Ovid: OV-id
Pactolus: pak-TOE-luss
Pan: pan
Phrygia: FRIJ-ee-yuh
Poseidon: poe-SIE-dun
satyr: SAY-ter
Silenus: sie-LEE-nuss
Tmolus: T'MOE-luss